JUST JOKING! 1,001 JOKES TO CRACK YOU UP

COMPILED BY S.K. DUNN

Compiled by: S. K. Dunn

Illustrated by: Buck Jones

Designed by: Nancy Panaccione

an imprint of
■ SCHOLASTIC
www.scholastic.com

Scholastic and Tangerine Press and associated logos are trademarks of Scholastic Inc.

Published by Tangerine Press, an imprint of Scholastic Inc., 557 Broadway; New York, NY 10012

Scholastic Australia Pty. Ltd
Gosford NSW

Scholastic New Zealand Ltd.
Greenmount, Auckland

Scholastic Canada Ltd.
Markham, Ontario

10 9 8 7 6 5 4 3 2 1

ISBN-10: 0-545-03271-7

ISBN-13: 978-0-545-03271-1

Printed and bound in China

CONTENTS

4   In the Beginning

8   Door's for You!

20   E-I-E-I-Ohhhhhh!

28   Laughing Wildly

38   What's Buggin' You?

44   Move Over, Rover! Don't Get Huffy, Fluffy!

50   Sea Sick

54   A Fowl Humor

68   Zoo Business

75   Ghastly Giggles

95   On-the-Job Training

107   A Little Byte Here, a Little Byte There

114   Bombs Away

120   School Daze

129   A Trip to the Doctor

148   Tasteful Humor

156   Take Note

160   Outta this World

163   Riddle Me This

176   My Poor Cousin Ninny!

182   What's in a Name?

189   A Very Punny Story

194   Mixed Nuts

IN THE BEGINNING
BIG YUKS ABOUT DINOSAURS

Caveman #1: IS it true that a dinosaur can't attack me if I'm wearing a raincoat?

Caveman #2: That depends.
How fast can you run in a raincoat?

WHAT DO YOU get WHEN YOU CROSS
a DINOSAUR WITH fIREWORKS?

Dino-mite!

WHY DO DINOSAURS eat tHEIR fOOD RAW?

Because they don't know how to cook.

WHAT DO YOU CALL a bLIND DINOSAUR?

A Doyouthinkhesaurus.

Teacher: WHAT fOLLOWED tHE DINOSAURS?

Student: Their tails?

WHAT DO DINOSAURS USE to CUt DOWN tREES?

Dinosaws.

There were three dinosaurs stranded on a deserted island. One day the first dinosaur found a bottle in the water, and he pointed it out to the other dinosaurs. The dinosaurs raced out and got the bottle. When the bottle was opened, a genie came out. He gave them each one wish. The first dinosaur wished to be in his homeland and—clap!—he was gone. The second dinosaur wished the same as the first dinosaur and—clap!—he was gone, too. And the third dinosaur said, "Gee, it's going to be lonely here without them. I wish they were back!"

WHY DO TYRANNOSAURUS LIKE TO EAT SNOWMEN?
Because they melt in their mouths!

HOW DO YOU KNOW THAT A BRONTOSAURUS HAS BEEN IN YOUR HOUSE?
The cheese is missing from all the mousetraps.

HOW DO YOU KNOW A TYRANNOSAURUS HAS BEEN IN YOUR HOUSE?
The Brontosaurus is missing.

WHO PUTS BRACES ON WOOLLY MAMMOTHS?
The mastodontist.

WHY DID THE DINOSAURS BECOME EXTINCT?
They didn't floss.

HOW DO YOU BRUSH A T. REX'S TEETH?
Very carefully!

**WHAT DO YOU CALL A DINOSAUR
THAT SLEEPS ALL DAY?**
A dino-snore.

**WHAT'S THE DIFFERENCE BETWEEN
A PTERODACTYL AND A PARROT?**
You'd know if you ever let a pterodactyl
sit on your shoulder!

WHICH type of DINOSAUR COULD JUMP
HIGHER than a HOUSE?

Any kind! A house can't jump!

WHAT DO you CALL a DINOSAUR IN
a cowboy HAT AND boots?

Tyrannosaurus Tex.

WHAT DO you CALL a DINOSAUR that SMASHES
everything IN itS path?

Tyrannosaurus Wrecks.

WHAT waS T. rex'S favORite NuMbeR?

Ate.

WHY ARe theRe OLD DINOSAUR bones
IN tHe muSeuM?

Because there aren't any new ones.

DOOR'S FOR YOU!
FIND OUT WHO'S ON THE OTHER SIDE OF THESE KNOCK-KNOCK JOKES!

Knock Knock.
Who's there?
Little Old Lady!
Little Old
Lady who?
I didn't know
you could yodel!

Knock Knock.
Who's there?
Banana!

Knock Knock.
Who's there?
Banana!

Knock Knock.
Who's there?
Banana!

Knock Knock.
Who's there?
Orange!
Orange who?
Orange you glad
I didn't say
banana?!

Knock Knock.
Who's there?
Bacon!
Bacon who?
Bacon a cake
for your
birthday!

Knock Knock.
Who's there?
Barbara!
Barbara who?
Barbara black
sheep, have you
any wool?

Knock Knock.
Who's there?
Bean!
Bean who?
Bean there,
done that!

Knock Knock.
Who's there?
Bertha!
Bertha who?
Bertha-day
greetings!

Knock Knock.
Who's there?
Betty!
Betty who?
Betty ya' don't
know who this is!

Knock Knock.
Who's there?
Bjorn!
Bjorn who?
Bjorn Free!

Knock Knock.
Who's there?
Bolivia!
Bolivia who?
Bolivia me,
I know what
I'm talking
about!

Knock Knock.
Who's there?
Boo!
Boo who?
Don't cry;
it's only a joke!

8

Knock Knock.
Who's there?
Butcher!
Butcher who?
Butcher money
where your
mouth is!

Knock Knock.
Who's there?
Candice!
Candice who?
Candice get any
better?

Knock Knock.
Who's there?
Candy!
Candy who?
Candy cow jump
over the moon?

Knock Knock.
Who's there?
Cash!
Cash who?
Cash me if you
can!

Knock Knock.
Who's there?
Celeste!
Celeste who?
Celeste time I'm
going to tell
you this!

Knock Knock.
Who's there?
Cello!
Cello who?
Cello 'dere!

Knock Knock.
Who's there?
Cereal!
Cereal who?
Cereal pleasure
to meet you!

Knock Knock.
Who's there?
Collin!
Collin who?
Collin me names
won't help!

Knock Knock.
Who's there?
Cynthia!
Cynthia who?
Cynthia been
away,
I missed you!

Knock Knock.
Who's there?
Daryl!
Daryl who?
Daryl never be
another you!

Knock Knock.
Who's there?
Diane!
Diane who?
Diane to meet
you!

Knock Knock.
Who's there?
Disguise!
Disguise who?
Disguise the
limit!

9

Knock Knock.
Who's there?
Duane!
Duane who?
Duane the bath,
I'm dwowning!

Knock Knock.
Who's there?
Earl!
Earl who?
Earl be glad to
tell you when you
open this door!

Knock Knock.
Who's there?
Aardvark!
Aardvark who?
Aardvark a
hundred miles
for one of your
smiles!

Knock Knock.
Who's there?
Aaron!
Aaron who?
Aaron on the side
of caution!

Knock Knock.
Who's there?
Abbott!
Abbott who?
Abbott time you
answered the
door!

Knock Knock.
Who's there?
Abe!
Abe who?
Abe C D E F G...

Knock Knock.
Who's there?
Abyssinia!
Abyssinia who?
Abyssinia later.

Knock Knock.
Who's there?
Acid!
Acid who?
Acid down and
be quiet!

Knock Knock.
Who's there?
Ada!
Ada who?
Ada burger for
lunch!

Knock Knock.
Who's there?
Adair!
Adair who?
Adair once but
I'm bald now!

Knock Knock.
Who's there?
Adelia!
Adelia who?
Adelia the cards
and we'll play Go
Fish!

Knock Knock.
Who's there?
Adlai!
Adlai who?
Adlai a bet on
that!

Knock, knock.
Who's there?
Adolf!
Adolf who?
Adolph ball hit
me in de mowf.
Dat's why I dawk
dis way!

Knock Knock.
Who's there?
Ahmed!
Ahmed who?
Ahmedeus Mozart!

Knock Knock.
Who's there?
Alaska!
Alaska who?
Alaska my friend
the question
then!

Knock Knock.
Who's there?
Al!
Al who?
Al give you the
answer if you
open this door!

Knock Knock.
Who's there?
Alba!
Alba who?
Alba in the
kitchen if you
need me!

Knock Knock.
Who's there?
Albee!
Albee who?
Albee a monkey's
uncle!

Knock Knock.
Who's there?
Albert!
Albert who?
Albert you don't
know who this is!

Knock Knock.
Who's there?
Alberta!
Alberta who?
Alberta'll be
over in a minute!

Knock Knock.
Who's there?
Alda!
Alda who?
Alda time you
knew who it was!

Knock Knock.
Who's there?
Aldo!
Aldo who?
Aldo anywhere
with you!

Knock Knock.
Who's there?
Alec!
Alec who?
Alec-tricity.
Isn't that a
shock?

KNOCK KNOCK.
WHO'S THERE?
ALEX!
ALEX WHO?
ALEX THE
QUESTIONS AROUND
HERE!

KNOCK KNOCK.
WHO'S THERE?
ALEXA!
ALEXA WHO?
ALEXA AGAIN TO
OPEN THIS DOOR!

KNOCK KNOCK.
WHO'S THERE?
ALFRED!
ALFRED WHO?
ALFRED THE NEEDLE
IF YOU SEW!

KNOCK KNOCK.
WHO'S THERE?
ALI!
ALI WHO?
ALI, ALI OXEN
FREE!

KNOCK KNOCK.
WHO'S THERE?
ALPACA!
ALPACA WHO?
ALPACA THE TRUNK,
YOU PACKA THE
SUITCASE!

KNOCK KNOCK.
WHO'S THERE?
AMAHL!
AMAHL WHO?
AMAHL SHOOK UP!

KNOCK KNOCK.
WHO'S THERE?
AMMONIA!
AMMONIA WHO?
AMMONIA LITTLE
KID!

KNOCK KNOCK.
WHO'S THERE?
AMORY!
AMORY WHO?
AMORY CHRISTMAS
AND A HAPPY NEW
YEAR!

KNOCK KNOCK.
WHO'S THERE?
ANDREW!
ANDREW WHO?
ANDREW A PICTURE!

KNOCK KNOCK.
WHO'S THERE?
ANDY!
ANDY WHO?
ANDY MOSQUITO
BIT ME AGAIN!

KNOCK KNOCK.
WHO'S THERE?
ANITA!
ANITA WHO?
ANITA YOU LIKE I
NEED A HOLE IN THE
HEAD!

KNOCK KNOCK.
WHO'S THERE?
ARNOLD!
ARNOLD WHO?
ARNOLD FRIEND YOU
HAVEN'T SEEN FOR
YEARS!

Knock Knock.
Who's there?
Thistle.
Thistle who?
Thistle have to
hold you until
dinner's ready.

Knock Knock.
Who's there?
I love.
I love who?
I don't know, you
tell me!

Knock Knock.
Who's there?
Police.
Police who?
Police stop
telling knock-
knock jokes!

Knock Knock.
Who's there?
Mary Lee.
Mary Lee who?
Mary Lee we roll
along.

Knock Knock.
Who's there?
Easter.
Easter who?
Easter anyone
inside who can
open the door?

Knock Knock.
Who's there?
Moira.
Moira who?
Moira Easter
Bunnies.

Knock Knock.
Who's there?
Howie.
Howie who?
Howie gonna get
rid of all these
Easter Bunnies?

Knock Knock.
Who's there?
Cargo.
Cargo who?
Cargo vroom
vroom.

Knock Knock.
Who's there?
Woo.
Woo who?
Don't get so
excited; it's just
a joke!

Knock Knock.
Who's there?
Who.
Who who?
Is there an owl
in here?

Knock Knock.
Who's there?
A little girl.
A little girl who?
A little girl who
can't reach the
doorbell.

Knock Knock.
Who's there?
Ivan.
Ivan who?
Ivan to suck your
blood!

Knock Knock.
Who's there?
Gorilla.
Gorilla who?
Gorilla me a
hamburger; I'm
hungry.

Knock Knock.
Who's there?
Cow go.
Cow go who?
No, cow go MOO!

Knock Knock.
Who's there?
Lettuce.
Lettuce who?
Lettuce in!

Knock Knock.
Who's there?
Max.
Max who?
Max no difference.

Knock Knock.
Who's there?
Police.
Police who?
Police let us in;
it's cold out here.

Knock Knock.
Who's there?
Norma Lee.
Norma Lee who?
Norma Lee I
don't go around
knocking on doors,
but do you want
to buy a set of
encyclopedias?

Knock Knock.
Who's there?
Dishes.
Dishes who?
Dishes me. Who ish
you?

Knock Knock.
Who's there?
Eileen.
Eileen who?
Eileen down to tie
my shoe.

Knock Knock.
Who's there?
Tarzan.
Tarzan who?
Tarzan stripes
forever.

Knock Knock.
Who's there?
Wendy.
Wendy who?
Wendy wind blows,
de cradle will rock.

Knock Knock.
Who's there?
Sara.
Sara who?
Sara doctor in
the house?

Knock Knock.
Who's there?
Yule.
Yule who?
Yule never know.

Knock Knock.
Who's there?
Hawaii.
Hawaii who?
I'm fine; Hawaii
you?

Knock Knock.
Who's there?
Anita.
Anita who?
Anita borrow
a pencil!

Knock Knock.
Who's there?
Olive.
Olive who?
Olive across the
road from you!

Knock Knock.
Who's there?
Luck.
Luck who?
Luck through
the keyhole and
you'll find out.

Knock Knock.
Who's there?
Phyllis.
Phyllis who?
Phyllis up a cup
of water!

Knock Knock.
Who's there?
Repeat.
Repeat who?
Who, who, who!

Knock Knock.
Who's there?
Mama.
Mama who?
Mama, please
open the door!

Knock Knock.
Who's there?
One shoe.
One shoe who?
One shoe open the
door, you'll find
out!

Knock Knock.
Who's there?
Goat.
Goat who?
Goat to the door
and find out!

Knock Knock.
Who's there?
Dexter.
Dexter who?
Dexter halls with
boughs of holly.

Knock Knock.
Who's there?
Danielle.
Danielle who?
Danielle, I can
hear you!

Knock Knock.
Who's there?
Tennis.
Tennis who?
Tennis-see!

Knock Knock.
Who's there?
Boo.
Boo who?
Don't cry—it's
only me!

Knock Knock.
Who's there?
Olive.
Olive who?
Olive you!

Knock Knock.
Who's there?
Pecan.
Pecan who?
Pecan someone
your own size!

Knock Knock.
Who's there?
Annie.
Annie who?
Annie thing you
can do, I can do
better.

Knock Knock.
Who's there?
Andrew.
Andrew who?
Andrew all over
the wall!

Knock Knock.
Who's there?
Dot.
Dot who?
Dots for me to
know, and you to
find out.

Knock Knock.
Who's there?
Icon.
Icon who?
Icon tell you
another knock-
knock joke. Do
you want me to?

Knock Knock.
Who's there?
Closure.
Closure who?
Closure mouth
when you're
eating!

Knock Knock.
Who's there?
Icy.
Icy who?
I see your
underwear!

HA HA HA HA
HA HA HA!!!

Knock Knock.
Who's there?
Nobel.
Nobel who?
Nobel, so I'll knock.

Knock Knock.
Who's there?
Radio.
Radio who?
Radio not, here I come!

Knock Knock.
Who's there?
Ya.
Ya who?
What are you getting so excited about?

Knock Knock.
Who's there?
Pencil.
Pencil who?
Pencil fall down if you don't have a belt.

Knock Knock.
Who's there?
Ice cream.
Ice cream who?
Ice cream every time I see a mouse.

Knock Knock.
Who's there?
Cash.
Cash who?
No, thanks. I prefer peanuts.

Knock Knock.
Who's there?
Accordion.
Accordion who?
Accordion to the TV, it's going to rain tomorrow.

Knock Knock.
Who's there?
Dime.
Dime who?
Dime to tell another knock-knock joke.

Knock Knock.
Who's there?
Butter.
Butter who?
I butter not tell you.

Knock Knock.
Who's there?
Omelet.
Omelet who?
Omelet smarter than I look!

Knock Knock.
Who's there?
Bow.
Bow who?
Not bow who; bow wow!

Knock Knock.
Who's there?
Tank.
Tank who?
You're welcome!

Knock Knock.
Who's there?
Who.
Who who?
You don't who;
owls do!

Knock Knock.
Who's there?
Doris.
Doris who?
Doris open. Come
on in.

Knock Knock.
Who's there?
Water.
Water who?
Water you doing
in my house?

Knock Knock.
Who's there?
Isabelle.
Isabelle who?
Isabelle
necessary on the
door?

Knock Knock.
Who's there?
Lettuce.
Lettuce who?
Lettuce be
friends!

Knock Knock.
Who's there?
Pig.
Pig who?
Pig up your feet
or you'll trip!

Knock Knock.
Who's there?
Ketchup.
Ketchup who?
Ketchup to me
and I will tell
you.

Knock Knock.
Who's there?
Water.
Water who?
Water you
answering the
door for?

Will you know me
tomorrow?
Yes.
Will you know me
next week?
Yes.
Will you know me
next year?
Yes.
Will you know me
in two years?
Yes.
Knock Knock.
Who's there?
I thought you
said you'd know
me!

Knock Knock.
Who's there?
Daisy.
Daisy who?
Daisy plays,
nights he sleeps!

KNOCK KNOCK.
WHO'S THERE?
THEODORE.
THEODORE WHO?
THEODORE IS STUCK
AND IT WON'T
CLOSE.

KNOCK KNOCK.
WHO'S THERE?
ARGUE.
ARGUE WHO?
ARGUE GOING TO
LET ME IN OR NOT?

KNOCK KNOCK.
WHO'S THERE?
MOO.
MOO WHO?
WELL, MAKE UP
YOUR MIND: ARE
YOU A COW OR
AN OWL?

KNOCK KNOCK.
WHO'S THERE?
CARGO.
CARGO WHO?
CARGO DOWN THE
ROAD.

KNOCK KNOCK.
WHO'S THERE?
VITAMIN.
VITAMIN WHO?
VITAMIN FOR A
PARTY!

KNOCK KNOCK.
WHO'S THERE?
TOBY.
TOBY WHO?
TOBY OR NOT
TO BE!

KNOCK KNOCK.
WHO'S THERE?
DEWEY.
DEWEY WHO?
DEWEY HAVE TO
KEEP TELLING
THESE KNOCK-
KNOCK JOKES?

KNOCK KNOCK.
WHO'S THERE?
CANDACE.
CANDACE WHO?
CANDACE BE THE
LAST KNOCK-KNOCK
JOKE?

E-I-E-I-OHHHHHH!
HEAD DOWN TO THE FARM
FOR SOME BARNYARD FUNNIES.

WHAT DO YOU GIVE A PIG WITH A RASH?
Oinkment!

WHERE DO SHEEP GET A HAIRCUT?
The bah-bah shop.

WHAT DO YOU GET IF YOU CROSS A CHICKEN WITH A COW?
Roost beef!

WHY DID THE PIG MOVE TO THE CITY?
He wanted to live in a styscraper.

What do you get from nervous cows?
Milkshakes.

Why are cows such bad dancers?
Because they have two left feet.

What do you get if you cross a rooster with a duck?
A bird that wakes you up at the quack of dawn.

Why do bulls wear bells?
Because their horns don't work.

What's a chicken's favorite game?
Hide and go peep.

Why do horses wear metal shoes?
Because sandals don't fit.

What do you call two cows in a tug of war?
Beef jerky.

Where do cows go for the best shopping?
Moo York.

What do you get when you cross a pig with a centipede?
Bacon and legs.

What goes "Oooo, oooo, oooo?"
A cow with no lips.

Teacher: What does the cow say?
Student: Moo.

Teacher: What does the cat say?
Student: Meow.

Teacher: What does the mouse say?
Student: Uh...Click?

What do you get if you cross a cow
with an octopus?
Something that can milk itself.

What do you call a sleeping bull?
A bull dozer.

What do you get when you cross a cow
with a volcano?
An udder disaster!

Why did the horse wake up in the middle
of the night?
She had a nightmare.

Where do baby cows go for lunch?
A calf-eteria.

How does a ram call his daughter to dinner?
"Hey, ewe!"

What do you do for a pig who's had
a bad accident?
Call a ham-bulance.

Where do cows go on Saturday nights?
To the moooo-vies.

What do you get from cows in the winter?
Ice cream.

How do mice celebrate when they move
into a house?
With a mouse-warming party!

What do you get if you cross a hen with a dog?
Pooched eggs.

What is a horse's favorite game?
Stable tennis.

What position do pigs play in football?
Swinebacker.

Why did the pig get a sunburn?
He was bacon in the sun.

Bennie: Pssst...Wanna hear a dirty story?
Betty: Sure!
Bennie: A white horse fell in the mud!

A lady from Chicago and her son
were riding the train through Iowa
when she noticed some cows.
"Oh, look! A bunch of cows!" she remarked.

"Not a bunch; herd," her son said.

"Heard of what?"

"Herd of cows."

"Of course I've heard of cows," she said.

"No, a cow herd."

"What do I care what a cow heard? I have no
secrets to keep from a cow!"

Why do bulls have rings in their noses?
Because rings won't fit on their hooves.

LAUGHING WILDLY
JOKES ABOUT ANIMALS WHO LIVE OUTSIDE

How do you catch a squirrel?
Climb up a tree and act like a nut.

Why didn't the skunk study for the big test?
He figured he could just use his in-stinks!

What do you get if you cross a baby deer with a ghost?
Bamboo.

What do you get if you boil a hyena with carrots and celery?
Laughing stock!

What did the rabbit give to his girlfriend?
A 24-carrot ring.

What do you get if you cross a skunk with a hornet?
A smelling bee.

HOW DO YOU STOP A SKUNK FROM SMELLING?
Put a clothespin on his nose.

HOW DOES A SKUNK CALL HER MOTHER?
On a smellular phone.

WHAT DO YOU GET IF YOU CROSS A SABER-TOOTHED TIGER WITH A PARROT?
I don't know, but when it talks, you'd better listen!

WHAT TIME IS IT WHEN YOU SEE A HUNGRY BEAR?
Time to run!

WHAT KIND OF ANIMAL COMES OUT ONLY ON CLOUDY DAYS?
A reindeer.

What do you call a group of bunnies jumping backward?
A receding hareline.

How do you know that carrots are good for your eyes?
Ever seen a rabbit wearing glasses?

How do rabbits make decisions?
By choosing heads or tails.

What's gray with big ears and a big trunk?
A rabbit going on vacation.

Why was the baby snake crying?
He'd lost his rattle.

What did the porcupine have for lunch?
A hamburger with prickles.

How do mother bunnies take care
of their babies?
With tender loving carrots.

Why do snakes have forked tongues?
Because they can't use chopsticks.

How do skunks organize their library books?
By the Pewey Decimal System.

Why don't skunks say much in meetings?
They are creatures of pew words.

What did the judge say when the skunk came
to court?
"Odor in the court! Odor in the court!"

What do you call a bear caught in the rain?
A drizzly bear.

Why was the rabbit so sad?
She was having a bad hare day!

What did the beaver say to the tree?
"Nice gnawing you!"

What kind of books do skunks read?
Best-smellers.

What do you call a grizzly bear with no teeth?
A Gummy bear.

What did the mother buffalo say to her son before he went to school?
"Bison!"

What do rabbits say to each other once a year?
"Hoppy Birthday!"

What do you get when you cross a baby goat with a baby porcupine?
A very stuck-up kid.

Snake #1: Are we poisonous?
Snake #2: Why do you ask?
Snake #1: Because I just bit my lip!

What is a snake's best subject?
Hisssssssssssssssstory!

Why are bears always cold?
Because they're always in their bear feet!

Which snake is best at math?
The Adder.

How did the rabbit get to Australia?
He flew by hareplane.

What do frogs do with paper?
Rip-it!

How does a frog feel when he has a broken leg?
Unhoppy.

What happens when you mix a frog with a bathtub scrubby-mit?
A rubbit!

Why did the frog read Sherlock Holmes?
He liked a good croak and dagger.

What happened to the frog's car when his parking meter expired?
It got toad!

What do you call a frog that crosses the road,
jumps in a puddle, and crosses the road again?
A dirty double-crosser!

What did the boy bat say to the girl bat?
"Wanna hang around together?"

What is a frog's favorite time?
Leap year!

Why did the frog go to the mall?
Because he wanted to go hopping.

How do you confuse a frog?
Put it in a round bowl and tell it to take
a nap in the corner.

What does a frog say when it sees
something great?
"Toadly awesome!"

What is a frog's favorite game?
Croaket.

What did the frog order at McDonald's?
French flies and a diet Croak.

Why did the frog go to the hospital?
He needed a hopperation!

What do stylish frogs wear?
Jumpsuits!

**What did the frog do after
it heard a funny joke?**
It started to croak up!

Why did the frog hold up the bank?
He wanted to robbit.

Why are frogs such liars?
Because they are amFIBians.

What did the frog say to the fly?
"You are really starting to bug me!"

What do frogs drink?
Hot croak-o.

What kind of shoes do toads wear?
Open-toad sandals.

What do you get if you cross a frog with a small dog?
A croaker spaniel.

What did one frog say to another?
"Time's sure fun when you're havin' flies!"

Why did the chimp get in trouble at school?
He wouldn't stop monkeying around.

WHAT'S BUGGIN' YOU?
GET INSECTED WITH LAUGHTER
BY THESE JOKES ABOUT BUGS.

Why is the bee's hair sticky?
He uses a honey comb!

What do you call a mosquito looking for a ride?
An itch-hiker.

How do fireflies start a race?
"Ready...set...glow!"

What's the difference between a mosquito and a fly?
Try zipping up a mosquito.

Why did the centipede drop off the basketball team?
She took too long to tie her shoes.

What did one flea say to the other?
"Should we walk or take the dog?"

Where do bees go when they're sick?
To the waspital.

What do you call a bee that's hard to understand?
A mumble bee.

What did the ant do when she couldn't eat the whole sandwich on her own?
She hired an assist ant.

How does a firefly say goodbye?
"I'm glowing now...."

WHY DID THE FIREFLY FAIL SCHOOL?
He wasn't very bright.

WHY DID THE FLY FLY?
Because the spider spied her.

HOW DO YOU MEASURE A SPIDER'S INTELLIGENCE?
With a fly-q test!

**WHAT INSECT TALKS SO MUCH THAT IT TURNS
INTO A BUTTERFLY?**
A chatterpiller.

WHY DID THE BEES GO ON STRIKE?
They wanted more honey and shorter flowers.

WHAT DO YOU GET IF YOU CROSS ANTS AND TICKS?
Pretty silly antics.

What does a spider wear to get married?
A webbing dress.

What did the boy firefly say
to the girl firefly?
"I'm de-lighted to meet you!"

What do termites eat for breakfast?
Oakmeal.

What do you call a fly with no wings?
A walk.

Two fleas were running across the
top of a cereal packet.
"Why are we running so fast?" said one.
The second one answered, "Because it says
'Tear along the dotted line.'"

What did the romantic flea say?
"I love you aw-flea!"

How do you start an insect race?
"One, two, flea—Go!"

**What do you call a flea that
lives in a dufus' ear?**
A space invader!

What is the most faithful insect?
A flea; once they find someone they like,
they stick to them!

**What is the difference between a flea-bitten
dog and a bored visitor?**
One's going to itch, and the other is itching to go!

What do you call a cheerful flea?
A hop-timist!

What does the slug say when it slides down the wall?
"My, how slime flies!"

What insect runs away from everything?
A flea (flee)!

What do you call a Russian flea?
A Moscow-ito!

What did the clean dog say to the insect?
"Long time no flea!"

MOVE OVER, ROVER!
DON'T GET HUFFY, FLUFFY!
PRETTY GOOD ONES ABOUT ALL KINDS OF PETS

WHERE DOES A DOG PARK ITS CAR?

In a barking lot.

WHAT DO YOU GET IF YOU CROSS A CAT
WITH A PARROT?

A carrot!

WHAT DO YOU GET WHEN YOU CROSS A CAT
WITH A LEMON?

A sour puss.

WHY DID THE MAN BUY A JOKE BOOK FOR HIS DOG?

Because it was a dull-mation.

WHAT DO YOU CALL A DOG WITH A BONE
IN EACH EAR?

Anything you want—he can't hear you anyway.

**WHAT DO YOU GET WHEN YOU CROSS A CAT
WITH A MOUSE?**

An animal that spends all day chasing its tail.

WHAT'S A DOG'S FAVORITE DRINK?

Pupsie Cola.

WHAT DO DOGS EAT AT THE MOVIES?

Pup-corn.

WHAT KIND OF DOG LOVES TO GET ITS HAIR WASHED?

A shampoodle.

HOW IS A DOG LIKE A SHEEP?

They both have fleece.

**WHAT DO YOU GET WHEN YOU CROSS A DOG
WITH A TREE?**

Bark!

WHat do you call a Jeep crossed with a dog?
Land Rover.

WHat is the difference between a boy and his dog?
One wears jeans and a shirt, the other just pants!

WHat kind of dog has red and yellow stripes and smells like onions?
A hot dog.

WHat's the most artistic dog?
A Paint Bernard.

WHat happened when the dog went to the flea circus?
He stole the show!

Mother dog: How was your test?
Baby dog: Rough, rough.

Where do you find a no-legged dog?
Wherever you left him!

What do cats have for breakfast?
Mice Krispies.

How do dogs communicate?
By flea-mail.

WHAT DOES a cat SaY at tHE END
of a Saucer of MiLK?
"That's the last lap!"

WHAT KIND of Pizza DO DOGS eat?
Pupperoni.

WHERE DO Kittens get their mittens?
From catalogs.

How DO mice ceLebRate HaLLoween?
With a mousequerade party.

WHAT iS a DOG'S favoRite DaY?
Chewsday.

A cat walks into a restaurant, orders a tuna sandwich on a bagel, and quietly sits down to eat it.

A man at the next table saw this and was shocked.

When the waitress came over to take his order, he said, "Wow, did you see that! That was amazing!"

"It sure is!" said the waitress. "How they stay so trim is beyond me!"

WHY DID THE GIRL STAY HOME WHEN SHE HEARD IT WAS RAINING CATS AND DOGS?
She didn't want to step in a poodle!

WHAT KIND OF DOG CAN TELL TIME?
A watch dog.

HOW DO YOU SPELL MOUSETRAP WITH ONLY THREE LETTERS?
C-A-T.

SEA SICK
THERE'S SOMETHING FISHY ABOUT THESE JOKES.

What's the difference between a piano and a fish?

You can't tune a fish!

What kind of gum do whales chew?

Blubber gum.

Why did the whale cross the road?

To get to the other side.

Where do whales look up words?

In the Moby Dictionary.

What does the snail use to call his mom when he's going to be late?

A shellular phone.

WHat DO SHaRKS Have at COOKOutS?
Clamburgers.

WHat'S a SHaRK'S faVORite game?
Swallow the leader.

WHat DiD tHe OCeaN Say tO tHe SHORe?
Nothing; it just waved.

WHat LieS at tHe bOttOM Of tHe Sea aND biteS itS NaiLS?
A nervous shipwreck!

Why is it so easy to weigh fish?
They have their own scales.

What happens when you cross a great white shark with a cow?
I don't know...but I wouldn't want to milk it.

What kind of shark never eats women?
A man-eating shark!

What did the shark eat for lunch?
A peanut butter and jellyfish sandwich.

WHY ARE FISH SO SMART?
They spend a lot of time in schools.

WHAT DO YOU GET WHEN YOU GRADUATE FROM FISH SCHOOL?
A deep-loma.

WHY DID THE CRAB GET ARRESTED?
Because he was always pinching things.

WHAT DO WHALES EAT?
Fish and ships.

WHY DIDN'T THE FIDDLER CRAB SHARE HIS DESSERT?
He was just a little shellfish.

A FOWL HUMOR
THESE JOKES ARE TOTALLY FOR THE BIRDS!

What do parakeets have at the end of a meal?

An after-supper tweet.

What shape is like a lost parrot?

Polygon!

What do you get when you cross a parrot and a shark?

A bird that talks your ear off!

Why do hummingbirds hum?

Because they forgot the words!

What do you get if you cross a canary and a 50-foot-long snake?

A sing-a-long!

Where does a 500-pound canary sit?
Anywhere it wants!

What does a duck like to eat with soup?
Quackers!

Why did the owl say, "Tweet, tweet?"
Because she didn't give a hoot!

What books did the owl like?
Hoot-dunits!

Why does a flamingo stand on one leg?
Because if he lifted that leg off the ground,
he would fall down!

Where does a peacock go when it loses its tail?
A re-tail store!

What's yellow, weighs 1,000 pounds, and sings?
Two 500-pound canaries!

Which side of a parrot has the prettiest feathers?
The outside!

What do you give a sick bird?
Tweetment!

What did the 500-pound canary say?
"Here Kitty, Kitty!"

WHY DO bIRDS FLY SOUTH FOR THE WINTER?
Because it's too far to walk!

WHAT TYPE OF bIRD VISITS THE HOSPITAL?
An illegal (ill eagle).

WHY DO SEAGULLS LIVE NEAR THE SEA?
Because if they lived near the bay,
they would be called bagels!

WHAT HAPPENS WHEN A DUCK FLIES UPSIDE DOWN?
It quacks up!

A duck went into a fancy French restaurant and ordered everything on the menu. He sat and ate for more than three hours, making a big mess and keeping the staff way after hours.

Eventually, the manager approached the table and spoke to the duck: "Excuse me, sir, we really appreciate your business but it's getting late and..."

Angrily, the duck looked up and said, "Is this about my bill?"

WHICH ANIMAL GROWS DOWN?
A duck!

DID YOU HEAR THE STORY ABOUT THE PEACOCK?
No, but I heard it's a beautiful tale (tail)!

WHAT'S NOISIER THAN A WHOOPING CRANE?
A trumpeting swan!

What bird is with you at every meal?
A swallow!

What's smarter than a talking parrot?
A spelling bee!

Why can't a rooster ever get rich?
Because he works for chicken feed!

Parker: I'd like to buy some bird seed.
Clerk: How many birds do you have?
Parker: None! I want to grow some!

What do you call a crate of ducks?
A box of quackers!

What key won't open any door?
A turkey!

What bird is always sad?
The blue jay!

What flies and captures ships on the high seas?
Parrots of the Caribbean.

What happened when the owl lost his voice?
He didn't give a hoot.

What do you call a very smart duck?
A wise quacker.

What do you get if you cross a parrot
with a centipede?
A walkie talkie.

What do you call a penguin in the desert?
Lost.

Why did the turkey, chicken, and duck get
thrown off the bus?
For using fowl language.

After a long day of shopping, the cashier
asked Mrs. Duck, "Cash, check, or charge?"
Mrs. Duck: "Just put it on my bill."

What's orange and sounds like a parrot?
A carrot.

What do birds eat for breakfast?
Shredded tweet.

Debbie Duck: Why do you like your boyfriend so much?
Delilah Duck: He quacks me up!

What kind of bird should never guard the bank?
A robin.

What's the difference between a duck with one wing and a duck with two wings?
Why, that's a difference of a pinion!

What kind of bird can carry the most weight?
A crane!

What do you call a duck who robs banks?
A safe quacker.

Why don't chickens like to play baseball?
They hit too many fowl balls.

What type of birds live in Portugal?
Geese.

What do you call a bird that looks like its dad?

A chirp off the old beak.

Why couldn't the crow call home very often?

It was a long distance caw.

If a rooster lays an egg on the middle of a slanted roof, on which side will it fall?

Neither side—roosters don't lay eggs!

What do you call a hen out in the garden?

Chicken salad!

Why wouldn't the chick cross the road?

He was a little chicken.

What did the sick chicken say?
"I have the people-pox!"

Who tells the best chicken jokes?
Comedi-HENS!

How does a chicken mail a letter to her friend?
In a HEN-velope!

What is a chick after she's six days old?
Seven days old!

Why do hens lay eggs?
If they dropped them, they'd break!

How do baby birds learn how to fly?
They just wing it.

How do chickens bake a cake?
From scratch!

MOLLY: Why does your son say, "Cluck, cluck, cluck?"

Mrs. O'Leary: Because he thinks he's a chicken.

MOLLY: Why don't you tell him he's not a chicken?

Mrs. O'Leary: Because we need the eggs.

How do you tell if a chicken has
a broken leg?

Give it an eggs-ray.

What do you get when you cross a chicken
with a centipede?

Enough drumsticks for everyone!

What day do chickens hate the most?

Fry-day.

Why did the chicken cross the road?

To get to the other side!

ZOO BUSINESS
ROAR AT THESE JOKES ABOUT ANIMALS FROM THE ZOO.

How do you get down from an elephant?
You don't; you get down from a goose!

What time is it when an elephant sits on an alarm clock?
Time to get a new alarm clock!

When do kangaroos celebrate their birthdays?
During a leap year!

What's the best way to catch a monkey?
Climb a tree and act bananas.

What's the difference between an elephant and a mouse?
About a ton.

What kind of key can you find in a tree?
A monkey.

Why are elephants always on time for flights?
Because they always have their trunks with them.

What happened when the pandas escaped
from the zoo?
It was panda-monium.

Rhinoceros: Help me, doctor! I just ate
a joke book!
Doctor: What's the problem?
Rhinoceros: Well, now I feel kind of funny....

How does a lion say hello?
"Pleased to eat you!"

What do lions say before going hunting?
"Let us prey."

Lion: Help me, doctor! I just ate a priest and I keep throwing up!
Doctor: Well, it's hard to keep a good man down.

What do you call a lion all dressed up?
A dandy lion.

What do you call a flat camel?
Humphrey!

What do you get if you cross a fish with an elephant?
Swimming trunks.

WHAT DO YOU CALL AN ELEPHANT THAT NEVER WASHES?

A smellyphant.

WHY ARE ELEPHANTS SO WRINKLED?

It would take too long to iron them.

WHAT DO YOU GET IF YOU CROSS A PARROT WITH A CROCODILE?

An animal that can talk your ear off.

WHAT'S BLACK AND WHITE AND EATS LIKE A HORSE?

A zebra.

WHAT'S BLACK AND WHITE, BLACK AND WHITE, BLACK AND WHITE?

A panda chasing a zebra chasing a penguin.

WHAT ANIMAL SHOULD YOU NEVER PLAY CARDS WITH?

A cheetah.

Why Can't Leopards Hide?

They are always spotted.

How Do You Get Down From a Giraffe?

Weren't you paying attention?
You get down from a goose.

Why Did the Mother Leopard Send Her Children Out to Play?

She wanted the house to be spotless.

What Do You Call a Cobra Who Is Fun at Parties?

A snake charmer.

What Do You Get When You Cross a Snake With a Basketball?

A bouncing baby boa.

How Do Snakes Sign Love Letters?

"With hugs and kisses."

What is the chameleon's favorite movie?
The Lizard of Oz.

What's the difference between an elephant and a flea?
Elephants can have fleas, but fleas can't have elephants.

What do you call an elephant that flies?
A jumbo jet.

What time is it when a hippopotamus sits on a fence?
Time to get a new fence.

What's black and white and black and white and black and white?
A zebra chasing a soccer ball.

What do you do when an elephant
stubs his toe?
Call a toe truck!

What do you call a mouse that hangs
around with boa constrictors?
Lunch.

What do pandas wear in their hair?
Bearrettes.

What do you get if you cross a hedgehog
with a giraffe?
A 10-foot brush.

How do you make an elephant sleep?
Give it a trunk-quilizer.

GHASTLY GIGGLES
JOKES ABOUT MONSTERS, WITCHES, GOBLINS, AND GHOULS

WHAT DID THE SKELETON SAY TO THE WAITER?
"I'll have the soup du jour and a mop."

WHY DO GHOSTS AND DEMONS ALWAYS GET ALONG WELL?
Because demons are a ghoul's best friend.

WHY ARE VAMPIRES SO GOOD AT WORD PROCESSING?
Because they always catch the type-Os!

WHO DOES A VAMPIRE FALL IN LOVE WITH?
The girl necks-door.

WHAT SPORT DO VAMPIRES LOVE?
Batmitten.

What's ugly and bounces up and down?
A witch on a trampoline.

Why are graveyards so loud?
Because of all the coffin.

Why can't people who live next to a graveyard be buried there?
Because they're not dead.

What's a monster's favorite TV show?
"Fiends."

Where do monsters learn algebra?
High sghoul.

What monster ate the Three Bears' porridge?
Ghouldilocks.

What street do monsters live on?
Dead ends.

What did the mother ghost say to the baby ghost?
"Don't spook until spooken to."

Why did the vampire go to the fish market?
He was looking for a sole!

What do you call a wizard from outer space?
A flying sorcerer.

WHy was tHe skeleton afraid to cross
the road?

It had no guts.

How do witches keep their hair in place
while flying?

With scare spray.

What did Dracula say when he kissed his
vampire girlfriend?

"Ouch!"

How do monsters tell their future?
They read their horrorscope.

What do you get when you cross a werewolf and a vampire?
A fur coat that fangs around your neck.

Do zombies eat popcorn with their fingers?
No, they eat the fingers separately!

Why don't skeletons ever go out on the town?
Because they don't have any body to go out with!

What do ghosts add to their morning cereal?
Booberries.

What do zombies like to eat at a cookout?
Halloweenies.

What is a vampire's favorite sport?
Casketball.

What is a vampire's favorite holiday?
Fangsgiving.

On which day do ghosts play practical jokes?
April Boo's Day.

Why did the vampire go to the orthodontist?
To improve his bite.

What do you get when you cross a vampire and a snowman?
Frostbite.

WHat does a ghost get when He falls and scrapes His knee?
A boo boo.

WHy do witches use brooms to fly?
Because vacuum cleaners are too heavy.

WHat is Dracula's favorite kind of coffee?
Decoffinated.

WHat do you call a classroom full of monsters?
Little ghouls and boo-ys!

WHat would a monster's psychiatrist be called?
Shrinkenstein.

What is a baby ghost's favorite game?
Peekaboo.

What did one ghost say to the other ghost?
"Do you believe in people?"

What do you call someone who puts poison
in a person's cornflakes?
A cereal killer.

Why do mummies have trouble keeping friends?
They're too wrapped up in themselves.

What does the papa ghost say to his family when driving?

"Fasten your sheet belts."

What do ghouls eat for breakfast?

Ghost toasties with evaporated milk.

What is a vampire's favorite mode of transportation?

A blood vessel.

What is a ghost's favorite mode of transportation?

A scareplane.

What type of dog do vampires like best?
Bloodhounds.

What is a ghoul's favorite flavor?
Lemon-slime.

A boy spending the night in a haunted house ran into a ghost.
The ghost told him, "I've been haunting this house for 200 years!"
The boy looked at the ghost and said, "In that case, can you tell me where the bathroom is?"

What does a vampire never order at a restaurant?
A stake sandwich.

What is a skeleton's favorite musical instrument?

A trombone.

What did the bird give out on Halloween night?
Tweets.

Why do vampires need mouthwash?
They have bat breath!

What's a vampire's favorite fast food?
A person with very high blood pressure!

Why did the vampire subscribe to *The Wall Street Journal*?
He heard it had great circulation.

Did you hear about the unlucky cannibal boy?
He was 8 before he was 7.

Did you hear about the cannibal who was expelled from school?

He was buttering up his teacher.

What does a cannibal get when he comes home late for dinner?

The cold shoulder.

What kind of car does a ghost drive?

A Boo-ick.

What do goblins drink at picnics?

Demonade.

What do ghosts use to wash their hair?

Sham-boo.

What kind of pants do ghosts wear?
Boo jeans.

Why wasn't the vampire working?
He was on a coffin-break.

What do skeletons say before eating?
"Bone appétit!"

What does a child monster call his parents?
Mummy and Deady.

Where do fashionable ghosts shop for sheets?
At bootiques.

What ride do spirits like best at the amusement park?
The roller ghoster.

What do you get when you cross a ghost with an owl?
Something that scares people and doesn't give a hoot.

What fairy tale do ghosts like best?
"The Emperor's Boo Clothes."

What kind of spirits serve food on a plane?
Airline ghostesses.

What kinds of ghosts haunt skyscrapers?
High spirits.

WHY DID THE SKELETON CLIMB A TREE?
Because a dog was after its bones.

HOW DO YOU MAKE A WITCH SCRATCH?
Just take away the W!

WHERE DO GHOSTS GO SWIMMING?
The Dead Sea.

WHY WAS THE WITCH'S CAT GIGGLING?
Because it was a giggle puss.

WHAT DO YOU DO WHEN 50 ZOMBIES
SURROUND YOUR HOUSE?
Hope it's Halloween.

WHaT DO you caLL a SKELeToN
SToNe Age famiLy?
The Flintbones.

WHaT DiD THe WiTcH Say to THe
miDgeT VamPire SKELeToN?
"Bony little bloodsucker, aren't you?"

WHaT'S THe DiffereNce betweeN a fiSHermaN
aND a SiCK gHoST?
One catches his dinner,
the other one loses it.

WHO DiD THe DOg DReSS uP aS for HaLLoweeN?
Hairy Pawter.

What is a vampire's favorite ice cream flavor?
Veinilla.

What kind of monster is extremely cautious?
A wary wolf.

What do you give a vampire with a cold?
Coffindrops.

Why did the vampires cancel their baseball game?
They couldn't find their bats.

WHAT DO YOU GET WHEN YOU DIVIDE
THE CIRCUMFERENCE OF A JACK-O-LANTERN
BY ITS DIAMETER?
Pumpkin pi.

WHICH MONSTER LIKES TO FLY KITES IN THE RAIN?
Benjamin Franklinstein.

WHAT DID THE MUMMY SAY TO THE DETECTIVE?
"Let's wrap this case up!"

WHY WAS THE WITCH KICKED OUT OF
WITCHING SCHOOL?
Because she flunked spelling.

WHEN A WITCH LANDS AFTER FLYING,
WHERE DOES SHE PARK?
The broom closet.

WHY CAN'T SKELETONS PLAY MUSIC IN CHURCH?
Because they have no organs.

HOW DO YOU TELL TWIN WITCHES APART?
You can't tell which witch is which!

WHAT DO YOU CALL A DEAD CHICKEN THAT LIKES TO SCARE PEOPLE?
A poultrygeist.

WHY DID THE MONSTER CROSS THE ROAD?
To eat the chicken!

WHAT'S THE DIFFERENCE BETWEEN SHREK AND A BOWL OF CARROTS?
One's a funny beast and the other's a bunny feast.

ON-THE-JOB TRAINING
SERIOUS FUNNY BUSINESS ABOUT WORK

HOW DO SCIENTISTS GET FRESH BREATH?
With experi-mints.

HOW DOES A BAKER MAKE HIS HOUSE PRETTY?
With a flour garden!

WHAT DID THE COFFEE SHOP MANAGER POST IN THE EMPLOYEE'S LOUNGE?
A list of dos and donuts.

WHAT DO GARBAGE MEN EAT?
Junk food!

WHAT DID THE TAILOR SAY TO THE MAN WHO FIRED HIM?
"Well, suit yourself."

WHY ARE bAKERS SO MEAN?
Because they whip the cream, beat the eggs,
and mash the potatoes.

WHY DID tHE fARMER bURY HIS MONEY?
He wanted to see it grow!

WHAt DID ONE MILKMAID SAY tO HER SIStER?
"You'll just have to wait your churn!"

WHY DID tHE MAN fREEZE HIS MONEY?
He needed cold hard cash.

WHY DID tHE tEDDY bEAR gO tO tHE DOCtOR?
Because he was all stuffed up!

WHAt ARE DENtIStS' twO fAVORItE LEttERS?
D-K (decay).

Why didn't the cannibal eat the weather forecaster?
He didn't want to catch a cold!

What did the doctor say to the curtains?
"Pull yourself together!"

What time should you go to the dentist?
Tooth-hurty!

Why do firefighters wear red suspenders?
To keep their pants up!

Why did the trombone player lose her job?
She kept letting her work slide.

Why did the writer spend all of her time cleaning the basement?
She was hoping for a best cellar!

Why did the butcher get fired?
He got caught choplifting.

What made the plumber cry?
When he saw his profits going down the drain.

Why was the broom late for work?
He overswept.

How does the barber send his letters?
Hair mail.

How do farmers fix their jeans?
With a cabbage patch.

Did the elevator operator like her job?
It had its ups and downs.

How did the carpenter chip his tooth?
Biting his nails.

How many jugglers does it take to screw in a lightbulb?
One, but he uses at least three bulbs.

How do garbage men break up with their girlfriends?
They dump them.

Did you hear that the fireman has a new girlfriend?
Well, actually, she's an old flame....

What is a plumber's favorite kind of shoes?
Clogs.

What is a gas station attendant's favorite kind of shoes?
Pumps.

What kind of shoes do lady golfers prefer?
Spike heels.

Where do secret agents get their groceries?
At the snooper market.

Why did the man quit his job at the eraser factory?
It rubbed him the wrong way.

How do ballerinas get into the city?
By tutu train.

Why did the lady quit her job as a coat maker?
It wore her out.

What is a perfume salesgirl's best quality?

She has good scents.

A policeman stops a lady and asks for her license. He says "Lady, it says here that you should be wearing glasses."

The woman answered, "Well, I have contacts."

The policeman replied, "I don't care who you know! You're getting a ticket!"

A tourist asks a man in uniform, "Are you a policeman?"

"No, I am an undercover detective."

"So why are you in uniform?"

"Today is my day off."

An unemployed man got a new job at the zoo. They offered to dress him up in a gorilla suit and pretend to be a gorilla so people would keep coming to the zoo.

On his first day on the job, the man put on the suit and went into the cage. The people all cheered to see him. He started putting on a show, jumping around, beating his chest, and roaring.

During one acrobatic attempt, though, he lost his balance and crashed through some safety netting, landing square in the middle of the lion cage! He lay there stunned, as the lion roared. Terrified, he screamed, "Help, help!"

The lion raced over to him, placed his paws on the man's chest and hissed, "Be quiet, or we'll both lose our jobs!"

A secretary was leaving the office one Friday evening when she encountered Mr. Jones, the human resources manager, standing in front of a shredder with a piece of paper in his hand.

"Listen," said Mr. Jones, "this is important, and my secretary has already left. Can you make this thing work?"

"Certainly," said the secretary. She turned the machine on, inserted the paper, and pressed the start button.

"Excellent, excellent!" said Mr. Jones as his paper disappeared inside the machine. "I just need one copy."

What were Tarzan's last words?
"Who greased the vine?!"

What do people do in clock factories?
They make faces all day.

Why did the tap dancer retire?
He kept falling in the sink.

One day the bank manager called a teller into her office. "I'm afraid we're going to have to let you go."

The teller was shocked. "But why?"

"Well, you keep giving away rolls of pennies to every person who comes in!"

The teller said, "But I thought that was just common cents!"

How does the biologist like to communicate?
With her cell phone!

Why did the rocket scientist lose his job?
He was fired!

Why did the dry cleaner leave the party early?
She had a pressing engagement.

Did you hear about the fire at the sneaker factory?
Over a hundred soles were lost!

Where do butchers go to dance?
The meat ball.

Why did the man at the orange juice factory lose his job?
He couldn't concentrate.

What do you get if you cross a burglar with a bag of cement?
A hardened criminal.

Why did the cleaning lady quit?
Because she figured out that grime doesn't pay.

Why did the baker stop making doughnuts?

He was sick of the hole business.

Zookeeper #1: We need you to take a census of all the monkeys in the world and report back to us.

Zookeeper #2: I'll need an ape recorder for that.

Why did the girl get fired from the bubble gum factory?

She'd bitten off more than she could chew!

A mathematician wandered home at 3 a.m. His wife became very upset, telling him, "You're late! You said you'd be home by 11:45!"

The mathematician calmly replied, "I'm right on time. I said I'd be home by a quarter of 12."

A Little Byte Here, a little Byte There

SOFT-BOILED HUMOR ABOUT TECHNOLOGY

What is a computer's first sign of old age?
Loss of memory.

What does a baby computer call his father?
Data.

What is a computer virus?
A terminal illness.

What do you do if your computer gets too hot?
Just open a window!

How do computers make sweaters?
On the interknit.

Why did the cat sit on the computer?
He was watching the mouse.

Customer: I bought a computer yesterday and there's a twig in the hard drive.
Salesperson: Sorry. You'll have to speak to the branch manager.

Did you hear about the monkey who left bits of his lunch all over the computer?
His dad went bananas.

Why did the vampire take a bite of the computer?
He wanted to go on the interneck.

What's in the middle of the World Wide Web?
A very big spider.

How did the computer get so fat?
Too many between-meal bytes.

Why do sheep have such big families?
To get more RAM.

WHY DID THE BOY PUT AN ELEPHANT ON HIS COMPUTER?

To get more memory.

HOW DO YOU CATCH A RUNAWAY COMPUTER?

With an internet.

WHAT'S A COMPUTER'S FAVORITE FOOD?

Chips.

Manny: THIS COMPUTER KEEPS ACTING UP!

Susan: Is it a Mac?

Manny: NO, it's a PC.

Susan: Are you sure?

Manny: YES! WHY?

Susan: Sounds like a crab Apple.

What makes a good computer programmer?
She always comes through when the chips are down.

Bennie: Why does your mother always put on a helmet before using your computer?
Betty: She heard they crash a lot.

Why was the computer tired after work?
It had a hard drive.

What do you get when you cross a computer with cottage cheese?
A curd processor.

Where do you send your computer for acting up?
Re-boot camp.

WHy DiD THe baby COMPuTeR CRy?
She wanted her motherboard.

WHy DiD THe COMPuTeR SKiP LuNCH?
She didn't like what was on the menu.

WHeRe DO COMPuTeR PROGRaMMeRS go foR weekeND getaways?
On a C: drive.

WHat DO you CaLL a COMPuTeR SuPeRHeRO?
A screen saver.

WHy DiD THe COMPuTeR CROSS THe ROaD?
To get a byte to eat.

WHO CHaSeS COMPuTeR CRiMiNaLS?
A hacker-tracker.

Proverb: Computer programmers don't byte, they nibble a bit.

Proverb: A picture's worth a thousand words, but it uses a thousand times more memory.

What do you get if you cross a computer with an elephant?

Lots of memory.

**WHat DO you get WHEN you cROSS a DOg
aND a coMPuteR?**
A machine that has a bark worse than its byte.

WHy waS tHe coMPuteR SO aNgRy?
Because it had a chip on its shoulder.

WHy DID tHe coMPuteR get glaSSeS?
To improve its web-sight.

WHy DID tHe coMPuteR SNeeze?
It had a virus.

WHeRe DO cOOL mIce LIve?
In mousepads.

BOMBS AWAY
SILLY AWAY MESSAGES FOR YOUR IM

A B C D E F G H I J K L M N O P Q
R S T V W X Y Z
oopz! i missed "U"

I went thataway ------->

Collecting myself...'cause I crack me up!

WORKING out. If I DON'T COME BACK, THEN
WHOEVER TOLD ME, "A LITTLE EXERCISE WON'T KILL
you," LIED.

You missed me; next time AIM better.

THIS SPACE FOR RENT.

Repetition is a sign of stupidity! Repetition is a sign of stupidity! Repetition is a sign of stupidity! Repetition is a sign of stupidity! Repetition is a....What was I saying again?

ON a scale of 1 to 10, I am a-weigh.

Let's discuss right and left.
You're right; I left.

HOME is WHERE you HANG youR @.

Experience is the hardest teacher;
it gives you the test first and then the lesson.

A JouRNey of a thousand sites begins
with a single click.

Don't byte off more than you can view.

You can't teach a new mouse old clicks.

Minds are like parachutes.
They work best when open.

It's no accident that stressed spelled
backward is desserts.

A chat has nine lives.

Give a man a fish and you feed him
for a day. Teach him to use the Net
and he won't bother you for weeks.

A friend is one who knows us,
but loves us anyway.

Roses are red,
Violets are blue,
Someone like you
Belongs in the zoo!

Don't get red,
Don't be blue,
Monkeys are
Silly, too!

Are you too gullible? Have $1,000?
We can cure you...click here.

UR 100% beautiful!
UR 100% lovely!
UR 100% sweet!
UR 100% nice!
...and UR 100% stupid
to believe these words!

I am studying procrastinating...leave a message.

I am a little spaced out right now;
be back when I am all together.

Did you hear the one about the person
who IMed someone and all he got was
an away message?

I hate my alarm clock...it works!

How can you miss me...if I didn't go away?

My dog ate my away message.

Pobody's Nerfect!

Rats! I forgot to leave an away message!

SCHOOL DAZE
A REAL CLASS ACT

What's the best way to get straight As?
Use a ruler.

Teacher: Can you tell me where the Grand Canyon is?
Student: Where was the last place you saw it?

Teacher: Why are you doing so poorly in school?
Student: Everything happened before I was born.

A student called in sick, pretending to be his father. The principal answered the phone.
"My son won't be in school today,"
the boy said in a deep voice.
Suspicious, the principal said,
"Young man, let me speak to your father."
The boy replied, "But this is my father!"

Teacher: Whitney, what's a Grecian urn?

Whitney: I think, with inflation, about $500 a week.

Teacher: How did the Vikings communicate?

Student: Norse code.

Teacher: You should be a printer.

Student: Why?

Teacher: You just seem like the right type.

121

Teacher: Why didn't you do your current events?

Student: I figured I'd wait until it was history.

Father: How was your test?

Son: Okay.

Father: Did the questions worry you?

Son: Well, not as much as my answers.

Teacher: What's the longest sentence you know?

Student: Life in prison?

Teacher: Give me a sentence with the word "analyze" in it.

Student: My sister Anna lies in bed until nine o'clock.

Teacher: Mary, why did you bring a picture of the Queen of Spain?

Mary: You told us to bring a ruler!

Teacher: Jack, can you please tell the class what two days of the week begin with the letter T?

Jack: Today and tomorrow?

Teacher: I told you to write a report on vegetables!

Student: I did—but my brother ate it!

Did you hear about the cross-eyed teacher?

She had no control over her pupils.

Teacher: Can anyone tell me the name of the explorer who sailed around the world to prove it was round?

Student: Sir Cumference?

Teacher: What do you know about the Iron Age?

Student: Sorry, I'm a bit rusty on that.

Teacher: JOHNNY, you are the worst-behaved student in my class!
Johnny: Yes, but I have the best attendance record.

Teacher: You're terrible at spelling and reading. Did you ever study your letters?
Student: Yes, but I always get stuck on two—T-V!

Student: My mother says we're descended from royalty.
Teacher: Who? The Burger King?

Teacher: Can anyone tell me three good reasons to be a teacher?
Student: June, July, and August.

Teacher: What do we call the study of the way societies spend their money?
Student: Buy-ology?

Principal: Someone stole the weighing machine from the nurse's office.
Teacher: I will launch a full-scale investigation.

Teacher: Please spell "wrong."
Student: R-O-N-G
Teacher: That's wrong!
Student: That's what you asked for!

Teacher: Can anyone tell me why the Eskimos eat raw fish and blubber?

Student: You would cry, too, if you had to eat raw fish.

Teacher: Why were the early days of history called the Dark Ages?

Student: Because there were so many knights!

What kind of food do math teachers eat?

Square meals!

Teacher: Can you tell me about the Ice Age?

Student: That's a slippery subject.

Teacher: I need you to pay a little attention!

Student: I'm paying as little as possible.

A TRIP TO THE DOCTOR
THIS GROUP MAY TEST YOUR PATIENTS!

Tricia: Help me, doctor! I was moving my computer, and now my back hurts.

Doctor: I think you may have slipped a disk.

Clark: Doctor, help me! My brother thinks he's a computer.

Doctor: Well, bring him in!

Clark: I can't. I need him to help with my homework.

Steve: Doctor, help me! My sister thinks she's a duck!

Doctor: Bring her in.

Steve: I can't; she's already flown south for the winter.

MOTHER: DOCTOR, HELP ME! MY SON THINKS HE'S a centipede!

Doctor: That's terrible!

MOTHER: AND THE WORST PART IS, HE JUST MADE THE BASKETBALL TEAM AND NEEDS NEW SHOES!

MOTHER: DOCTOR, PLEASE HELP ME. EVERY MORNING, MY DAUGHTER THINKS SHE'S THE EASTER BUNNY.

Doctor: Hmmm.

MOTHER: WHAT'S WORSE IS THAT SHE HIDES ALL MY EGGS THE NIGHT BEFORE.

JENNY: DOCTOR, I THINK MY BROTHER'S BUILT UPSIDE DOWN.

Doctor: Why's that?

JENNY: HIS NOSE RUNS AND HIS FEET SMELL!

Tom: Doctor, I'm suffering from amnesia!

Doctor: Go home and forget about it.

Mary: Doctor, sometimes I think I'm a trash can.

Doctor: Why, I've never heard such garbage!

Peter: Doctor, I've got bad breath, rotten teeth, and stinky feet.

Doctor: Sounds like you've got foot and mouth disease.

Shelly: Doctor, I think I'm a needle.

Doctor: I see your point.

THE COMEDIAN WENT TO THE DOCTOR. "DOC, YOU GOTTA HELP ME. I'VE BEEN SO WORRIED ABOUT LOSING MY JOB I CAN'T EAT OR SLEEP. NOW I FEEL FUNNY."

The doctor replied, "Well, maybe you should try to *sound funny*...."

AFTER A VERY BAD ACCIDENT, A RADISH RUSHED HIS WIFE TO THE HOSPITAL. HE ASKED THE DOCTOR, "CAN YOU SAVE HER?"

The doctor replied, "Well, yes, but I'm afraid she'll be a vegetable for the rest of her life."

FATHER: DOCTOR, MY SON SWALLOWED A ROLL OF FILM!

Doctor: Well, let's just wait and see what develops.

MOTHER: DOCTOR, HELP ME! MY DAUGHTER SWALLOWED A PEN.

Doctor: Well, use a pencil until I get there.

Betty: DOCTOR, I KEEP THINKING I'M A DOG.

Doctor: Sit up here on the couch and we'll talk.

Betty: OH, I'M NOT ALLOWED ON THE COUCH.

Jeff: DOCTOR, SOMETIMES I GET THE STRANGEST FEELING THAT I'M A BRIDGE.

Doctor: Interesting! Can you describe what's come over you?

Jeff: A TRUCK, A CAR, SOME MOTORCYCLES....

Francis: DOCTOR, I KEEP THINKING THERE ARE TWO OF ME.

Doctor: One at a time, please!

Bob: DOCTOR, I THINK I'M A MOTH.

Doctor: So, why did you come around then?

Bob: WELL, I SAW THIS LIGHT AT THE WINDOW!

Arnie: DOCTOR, HAVE YOU GOT SOMETHING FOR A BAD HEADACHE?

Doctor: Of course. Just take this hammer and hit yourself in the head. Then you'll have a bad headache.

Ann: DOCTOR, I FEEL LIKE A RACEHORSE.

Doctor: Take one of these every four laps!

Kevin: DOCTOR, MY SISTER HERE KEEPS THINKING SHE'S INVISIBLE!

Doctor: What sister?

Suzy: DOCTOR, I KEEP THINKING I'M INVISIBLE.

Doctor: Who said that?

ARNOLD: Doctor, I keep thinking I'm a snake about to shed its skin.

Doctor: Well, why don't you go behind the screen and slip into something more comfortable, then!

Sean: Doctor, I'm on a diet and it's making me irritable. Yesterday I bit someone's ear off.

Doctor: Oh dear; that's a lot of calories!

CHRISTY: Doctor, you have to help me out!

Doctor: Certainly. Which way did you come in?

WENDY: Doctor, can I have a second opinion?

Doctor: Of course—come back tomorrow!

MELANIE: Doctor, I think I'm a butterfly!

Doctor: Will you say what you mean and stop flitting about!

DOCTOR: You need new glasses!

Ralph: How do you know? I haven't told you what's wrong with me yet.

DOCTOR: I could tell as soon as you walked in through the window....

James: DOCTOR, I think I'm a snail.

Doctor: Don't worry; we'll soon have you out of your shell!

Heather: DOCTOR, I feel like an apple.

Doctor: We must get to the core of this!

Sharon: DOCTOR, I think I'm a pot of soup!

Doctor: Just simmer down!

Angie: DOCTOR, I THINK I'M AN ADDER.

Doctor: Great—can you help me with my accounts, please?

Diane: DOCTOR, I KEEP PAINTING MYSELF GOLD.

Doctor: Don't worry; it's just a gilt complex!

Murphy: DOCTOR, I'VE BROKEN MY ARM IN TWO PLACES.

Doctor: Well, don't go back there again!

Mike: DOCTOR, I THINK I'M A DOG.

Doctor: How long have you felt like this?

Mike: EVER SINCE I WAS A PUPPY!

Jason: DOCTOR, I FEEL LIKE A PACK OF CARDS.

Doctor: I'll deal with you later!

Burt: DOCTOR, I THINK I'M TURNING into a frog.

Doctor: You're just playing too much croquet!

Leslie: I THINK I'M a yo-yo.

Doctor: Are you just stringing me along?

Lisa: I DREAM THERE ARE MONSTERS UNDER my bed; what can I do?

Doctor: Saw the legs off your bed!

Jenny: DOCTOR, WHEN I PRESS WITH MY FINGER HERE, it HURTS. AND it HURTS HERE, HERE, AND HERE! WHAT DO YOU THINK IS WRONG WITH ME?

Doctor: You have a broken finger!

Bryan: Doctor, I feel as though I'm becoming invisible.

Doctor: Yes, I can see you're not all there!

Lenny: Doctor, I've just swallowed a pen!

Doctor: Well, sit down and write your name!

Drew: Doctor, I keep thinking I'm a frog.

Doctor: What's wrong with that?

Drew: I think I'm going to croak!

Janelle: Doctor, I snore so loud I keep myself awake.

Doctor: Sleep in another room then!

Gabby: DOCTOR, MY baby'S SWALLoweD a buLLeT!

Doctor: Well, don't point him at anyone until I get there!

JOHN: DOCTOR, I KeeP tHINKING I'M a vaMPiRe.

Doctor: Necks, please!

DaviD: How caN I cuRe My SLeePwaLKiNG?

Doctor: Sprinkle thumbtacks on your bedroom floor!

Rosa: DOCTOR, MY SiSTeR tHiNKS SHe'S aN eLevaTOR!

Doctor: Well, tell her to come in.

Rosa: I caN't—SHe DOeSN't StOP at tHiS fLOOR!

Claire: Doctor, everyone keeps
        ignoring me.
Doctor: Next, please!

Wife: My husband smells like fish!
Doctor: Poor sole!

Carl: Doctor, doctor,
      I've lost my memory!
Doctor: When did this happen?
Carl: When did what happen?

Kathy: I keep seeing double.
Doctor: Please sit on the couch.
Kathy: Which one?

Sylvia: DOCTOR, I'M A BURGLAR!

Doctor: Have you taken anything for it?

Kate: DOCTOR, I KEEP THINKING I'M A NIT.

Doctor: Will you get out of my hair?

Phil: DOCTOR, I KEEP THINKING I'M A CATERPILLAR.

Doctor: Don't worry; you'll soon change!

Amber: I'VE HAD A TUMMY ACHE SINCE I ATE THREE CRABS YESTERDAY.

Doctor: Did they smell bad when you took them out of their shells?

Amber: WHAT DO YOU MEAN, "...TOOK THEM OUT OF THEIR SHELLS"?

Emily: DOCTOR, everyone thinks I'm a liar.
Doctor: I can't believe that!

Martin: DOCTOR, I feel like a sheep.
Doctor: That's baaaaaaaaaad!

Monica: DOCTOR, I feel like a bee.
Doctor: Well, buzz off. I'm busy!

DOCTOR: I have some bad news and some very bad news.

Clarissa: Well, you might as well give me the bad news first.

DOCTOR: The lab called with your test results. They said you have 24 hours to live.

Clarissa: 24 HOURS! That's terrible! WHAT could be WORSE? What's the very bad news?

DOCTOR: I've been trying to reach you since yesterday.

The surgeon told his patient who woke up after having been operated on: "I'm afraid we're going to have to operate on you again. Because, you see, I forgot my rubber gloves inside you."
"Well, if that's the only reason," the patient said, "I'd rather pay for them and you can just leave me alone."

Wife: My husband thinks he's a satellite dish.

Doctor: Don't worry; I can cure him.

Wife: I don't want him cured. I want you to adjust him to get the movie channel.

Bob said to the X-ray technician after swallowing some money:
"Do you see any change in me?"

Nurse: Doctor, the man you've just treated collapsed on the front step. What should I do?

Doctor: Turn him around so it looks like he was just arriving!

Did you hear about the Siamese twins?
Everything goes in one ear and out the brother.

Did you hear about the man who fell into an upholstery machine?
He's fully recovered.

A mother complained to her doctor about her daughter's strange eating habits: "All day long she lies in bed and eats yeast and car wax. What will happen to her?"
"Eventually," said the doctor,
"she will rise and shine!"

A guy walked into work with his ears all bandaged up. The boss asked him, "What happened to your ears?"

"Yesterday I was ironing a shirt when the phone rang, and I accidentally answered the iron," he said.

"Well, that explains one ear, but what happened to your other ear?" his boss asked.

The guy responded, "Well, I had to call the doctor!"

Ron: Doctor, are you sure I'm suffering from pneumonia? I've heard once about a doctor treating someone with pneumonia, and he finally died of typhus.

Doctor: Don't worry; it won't happen to me. If I treat someone with pneumonia, he will die of pneumonia.

147

TASTEFUL HUMOR
JOKES ABOUT FOOD THAT WILL TICKLE YOUR RIBS

WHY IS MILK THE FASTEST THING IN THE WORLD?
Because it's pasteurized before you see it.

DID YOU HEAR ABOUT THE EGGS WHO WERE CAUGHT STEALING?
They were put into custardy.

WHAT DO YOU GET IF YOU CROSS A CHICKEN WITH A KANGAROO?
Pouched eggs.

HOW DO GHOSTS LIKE THEIR EGGS?
Terrifried.

WHAT DO YOU GET IF YOU CROSS A SPACESHIP WITH BACON?
An unidentified frying object.

How do you make a potato puff?
Chase it around the garden.

What did the leftover pizza say just before it went into the fridge?
"Curses! Foiled again!"

Why did the cookie get lonely?
She'd been a wafer too long.

How do the police take hamburgers to jail?
In a patty wagon.

What is the twins' favorite fruit?
Pears!

What do you call a million strawberries
trying to get through the door?
Strawberry jam!

Why did the lettuce turn red?
Because it saw the salad dressing!

What does a salad say before dinner?
"Lettuce pray!"

How do you fix a cracked pumpkin?
With a pumpkin patch!

What do you call two peas in a fight?
Black-eyed peas.

What vegetable shouldn't go on a boat?
A leek.

Where do vegetables go out after work?
A salad bar.

What's the strongest vegetable?
A muscle sprout.

What is the most dishonest fruit?
A lie-berry!

What did the banana say to his girlfriend?
"I find you quite appeeling!"

What vegetable is best at music?
A beet!

Did you hear the joke about the peach?
It was pitiful.

Did you hear about the corn in a fight?
He got creamed.

What's worse than finding a spider in your sandwich?
Finding half a spider in your sandwich.

What cheese is made backward?
Edam.

Customer: Waiter, this food tastes funny.
Waiter: Then why aren't you laughing?

What does the farmer say to the noisy vegetables?
"Could you peas be quiet?"

How are flip-flops like banana peels?
They're both easy to slip on.

Why don't bananas get lonely?
Because they hang in bunches!

Proverb: Ham and eggs are a quick breakfast for you, but a day's work for a chicken, and a lifetime commitment for a pig.

Proverb: Time flies like an arrow. Fruit flies like a banana.

Bennie: Did you hear the joke about
the broken egg?

Betty: Yes, it cracked me up!

Customer: Waiter, why don't you serve
spaghetti after 8 P.M.?

Waiter: Well, sir, it's pasta bedtime.

What's a scarecrow's favorite fruit?
Straw-berries!

Why isn't there ever a fight in the kitchen?
When the oven starts heating up and the pots
begin to boil, the refrigerator starts running and
the water goes down the drain.

Why are egg surgeons always so serious?
Because they know that if they just cut out all the
yolks, their patients will be all-white!

How do eggs like to fly?
Only first class—NEVER poach!

What do you call eggs who betray their country?
Eggs Benedict Arnold.

Why did the cabbage win the race?
Because it was a-head!

What did the mayonnaise say to the fridge?
"Close the door—I'm dressing!"

Why was the tomato last in the race?
It couldn't ketchup!

What kind of cheese is never for you?
Nacho cheese.

TAKE NOTE

JUST TRY TO TUNE OUT THESE
KNEE-SLAPPERS ABOUT MUSIC.

How Do you clean a flute?

With a tuba tootpaste.

Why did the girl bring a ladder to music class?

To reach the high notes!

Why was the balloon afraid to go
to the concert?

He heard it was all pop music!

Where did the music teacher leave her keys?

In the piano!

Why did the marching band stop washing
before the big game?

They wanted to be in-stink!

What instrument can you use to call your mother?
A sax-o-phone!

Why do you need a chicken in a band?
Because they bring their own drumsticks!

What kind of music do mummies love best?
Rap!

What's the loudest pet?
Trump-pet!

What's a computer's favorite music?
Disc-o.

WHAT KIND OF MUSIC DO FROGS LOVE BEST?
Hip-hop.

WHY DID THE TRUMPET GO TO THE DENTIST?
He needed a toot canal.

WHY ARE SKELETONS ALWAYS SO QUIET IN
MUSIC CLASS?
They don't have an organ.

WHY DON'T THEY JUST USE A PIANO?
There's no body to play it.

WHAT KIND OF INSTRUMENT COSTS
A THOUSAND DOLLARS?
A grand piano.

In what key do you play "Running with the Bulls"?
C sharp or B flat.

A note left for a pianist from his wife:
Gone Chopin, (have Liszt), Bach in a Minuet.

What do you get when you drop a piano down a mine shaft?
A flat minor.

What did the guitar say to the guitarist?
"Pick on someone your own size!"

What do you get when you cross a banjo with a chicken?
Something that plays a tune when you pluck it!

OUTTA THIS WORLD
FAR-OUT JOKES ABOUT OUTER SPACE

WHERE DO TRAINED ASTRONAUTS EAT THEIR LUNCH?
In the "launch" room.

WHY IS A MOON ROCK TASTIER THAN AN EARTH ROCK?
Because it is a little meteor (meatier)!

HOW DOES AN ASTRONAUT GET READY FOR A TRIP?
Plan it!

WHAT DID NEPTUNE SAY TO SATURN?
"Give me a ring sometime."

WHERE DO ASTRONAUTS LEAVE THEIR SPACESHIPS?
At parking meteors.

Marcia Martian: I was at a party on Mercury last night.

Martin Martian: Was it any good?

Marcia Martian: No! It was really boring.

Martin Martian: How come?

Marcia Martian: There was no atmosphere.

Astronaut #1: I'm hungry.

Astronaut #2: So am I. It must be launch time!

What HOLDS THE MOON UP?
Moon beams!

What KIND OF POEM CAN YOU FIND IN OUTER SPACE?
Uni-verse!

WHEN IS A WINDOW LIKE A STAR?
When it's a skylight!

What's A MARTIAN'S NORMAL eyesight?
20-20-20.

What KINDS OF SONGS DO PLANETS LIKE TO SING?
Nep-tunes!

How DO YOU GET A BABY ASTRONAUT TO SLEEP?
You rock-et!

RIDDLE ME THIS
MINI-WORKOUTS FOR YOUR BRAIN AND FUNNY BONE

WHAT GOES THROUGH A DOOR, BUT NEVER GOES IN OR OUT?

A keyhole.

WHAT'S THE FASTEST WAY TO WIDEN A ROAD?

Just add a B—then it becomes broad right away!

WHERE CAN YOU ALWAYS FIND MONEY?

In the dictionary.

WHAT CAN RUN, BUT CAN'T WALK?

Water.

WHAT HAS LOTS OF EARS, BUT CAN'T HEAR?

A cornfield.

Did you ever see a sidewalk?
Nope, but I've seen a lemonade stand.

Have you ever seen an engagement ring?
Nope, but I've seen a rubber band.

What has an eye, but can't wink?
A needle.

What has teeth, but can't bite?
A comb.

What has a bottom on its top?
A pair of legs.

What can you catch, but not throw?
A cold.

What can you throw, but not catch?
Your voice.

What's black and white and read all over?
A newspaper.

What's as big as an elephant, but weighs nothing?
An elephant's shadow.

During what month do people sleep the least?
February; it only has 28 days.

What are two things you can't have for breakfast?

Lunch and dinner.

What has eyes and a tongue, but can't see or taste?

A shoe.

What can you hear, but not see, and only speaks when spoken to?

An echo.

How many yo-yos fit in an empty box?

One—after that, the box won't be empty.

What is easier to give than receive?

Advice.

Does any word in the English language
contain all of the vowels?
Unquestionably!

What has eyes, but can't see?
A potato.

What do you put on a table and cut,
but not eat?
A deck of cards.

When does water stop flowing downhill?
When it reaches the bottom.

What word is always spelled incorrectly?
Incorrectly.

What's the last thing you take off
before going to bed?
Your feet off the floor.

What is always coming but never arrives?
Tomorrow.

What can you serve, but never eat?
A tennis ball.

What travels all over the world, even
though it stays in one place?
A postage stamp.

What do you put in a bucket full of water
to make it lighter?
A hole.

WHAT gets wetter the more you get dry?
A towel.

WHAT breaks every time someone speaks?
Silence.

WHAT goes all around a field,
but never moves?
A fence.

WHAT can you HOLD without touching?
Your breath.

WHAT starts with M, ends with X,
and HAS LOTS of LETTERS in it?
Mailbox.

WHat goes up aND DOWN, but never moves?

A flight of stairs.

How many seconds are there in a year?

Twelve—one every month (January 2, February 2, etc.).

WHicH candle burns longer: a blue one or a yellow one?

Neither—candles burn shorter, not longer.

What belongs to you, but is mostly used by otHer people?

Your name.

What kind of cup can't HOLD water?

A cupcake.

When things go wrong, what can you
always count on?
Your fingers.

What can you give and have at the same time?
A cold.

What has two hands but no fingers,
a face but no eyes, moves all the time,
but never leaves its spot?
A clock.

What's at the beginning of eternity, the end
of time, and the beginning of everything?
The letter E.

What can't walk, but runs very fast?
A river.

What grows more the less you see?
Darkness.

What is bigger when you turn it upside down?
The number 6.

If a man is born in France, moves to Italy,
gets married in Germany, but dies in China,
what is he?
Dead.

What goes through water, but never gets wet?
Sunlight.

What do you call a man who shaves
20 times a day?
A barber.

What's black when it's clean and white when it's dirty?

A chalkboard.

What weighs more, a pound of feathers or a pound of rocks?

They both weigh the same—one pound.

What's taken before you even see it?

Your picture.

What's the only question you can never answer?

"Are you asleep?"

What has lots of holes but holds a lot of water?

A sponge.

What flies all day, but never goes anywhere?
A flag.

What's easier to get into than it is
to get out of?
Trouble.

Why do parents dress baby girls in pink
and baby boys in blue?
Because babies can't dress themselves!

What occurs once every minute but
never in a year?
The letter M.

What has four legs and flies?
A picnic table.

What happens between sunrise and sunset?
Sunburn.

Can alligators have babies?
No, they have little alligators.

What five-letter word becomes shorter when you add two letters to it?
Short.

What's better than the best thing and worse than the worst thing?
Nothing.

What's the longest word?
"Smiles," because it has a mile between the first and last letters!

MY POOR COUSIN NINNY!

THE MISADVENTURES OF A NOT-SO-SMART RELATIVE

Abe: My poor cousin Ninny! He just lost his job in a restaurant!

Bea: How?

Abe: When someone told him the refrigerator was running, he went outside to catch it!

Abe: My poor cousin Ninny! He lost his job at the M&M factory.

Bea: Why?

Abe: He kept throwing away all the Ws!

My poor cousin Ninny! He missed the evening news because his radio was only AM.

My poor cousin Ninny! He climbed a chain link fence to see what was on the other side!

My POOR COUSIN NINNY! He THREW away all the bananas because He COULDN'T figure out How to get them OPEN.

Abe: My POOR COUSIN NINNY! He ONLY wants a BMW.

Bea: Why? Is he rich?

Abe: No, it's just the ONLY Name He can SPELL!

My POOR COUSIN NINNY! WHEN He OPENED a box of CHEERIOS, He THOUGHT it was DOUGHNUT SEEDS!

My POOR COUSIN NINNY! WHEN He fOUND SIX emPty MILK CARTONS, He thought it was a COW'S NEST!

Abe: My POOR COUSIN NINNY! He got a PROMOTION at WORK, but LOST HIS JOB the next day!

Bea: Why?

Abe: WHEN the BOSS came in the MORNING, NINNY HAD cut DOWN all the trees in FRONT of the building. AND WHEN they ASKED HIM WHY, He said, "I thought I was BRANCH Manager!"

Abe: My POOR cousin NINNY! He got THROWN off the water POLO team in COLLEGE.

Bea: Why?

Abe: HIS HORSES KEPt DROWNING!

Abe: My POOR cousin NINNETTE! SHe got THROWN off the field HOCKEY team.

Bea: Why?

Abe: Her SKateS KePt tearing up the field.

My poor cousin Ninny! He planted his iPod
so it would grow into a stereo system!

Abe: My poor cousin Ninny! He found a million
dollars and returned it to the police.

Bea: Why?

Abe: He thought it may have belonged to a
poor person.

Cousin Ninny: I'd like to buy 10 pounds of nails.

Clerk: That'll be $27, plus tax.

Cousin Ninny: No, no! I only want nails,
not tacks.

Abe: My poor cousin Ninny! He lost his
job as a manicurist!

Bea: How?

Abe: When someone asked to have her nails
filed, he asked if he should do it by size
or alphabetically.

Abe: My POOR COUSIN NiNNy! He LOST HiS JOB as a waiter!

Bea: How?

Abe: WHEN SOMEONE ASKED HiM to DRESS tHe SaLaD FOR DiNNER, He ASKED if it waS FORMAL!

Abe: My POOR COUSIN NiNNy! He LOST HiS JOB as a butLER!

Bea: How?

Abe: It took HiM aLL DAy to DRaw tHe DRaPeS because He KePt breaking HiS PeNCiL.

Abe: My POOR COUSIN NiNNy! He LOST HiS JOB as a baKER!

Bea: How?

Abe: WHEN He HEARD tHe DOUGH HaD to RiSE, He FLOODED tHe bakERy.

Abe: My poor cousin Ninny! He lost his job as a computer technician.

Bea: Why?

Abe: Every time someone brought in a MAC for repairs, he'd just throw them away!

Bea: Why?

Abe: He thought one bad APPLE could spoil the whole bunch.

Abe: My poor cousin Ninny! He lost his job as a barber!

Bea: How?

Abe: When a lady came in and asked for a haircut, he asked which one.

WHAT'S IN A NAME?
FUN WITH NAMES

What do you call a man who likes
to work out?

Jim.

What do you call a girl in the middle
of a tennis court?

Annette.

What do you call a woman standing on a hill?

Eileen.

What do you call a boy hanging on a wall?

Art.

What do you call a boy at the bottom
of a bathtub?

Dwayne.

What do you call a boy with a map on his head?

Miles.

What do you call a boy who can lift a car?
Jack.

What do you call a boy with a shovel?
Doug.

What do you call a boy without a shovel?
Douglas.

What do you call a boy in a pile of leaves?
Russell.

What do you call a girl singing at Christmas?
Carol.

What do you call a man who owes money?
Bill.

What do you call a man broadcaster?
Mike.

WHAT DO YOU CALL a boy tumbling DOWN a HiLL?
Roland.

WHAT DO YOU CALL a HaPPy girl?
Mary.

WHAT DO LawyeRS Name THeiR DaugHTeRS?
Sue.

WHAT DO YOU CALL a girl at THe beach?
Sandy.

WHAT DO YOU CALL a boy wHo can't Swim?
Bob.

WHAT DO YOU CALL a girl wHo SmeLLS good?
Rose.

WHAT DO YOU CALL a boy oN HiS way
to THe barber?
Harry.

What Do you call a boy in Spring?
Bud.

What Do you call a girl standing between two buildings?
Ally.

A pregnant woman from Washington, D.C., gets in a car accident and falls into a deep coma. Asleep for nearly six months, she wakes up to find that she is no longer pregnant. Frantically, she asks the doctor about her baby.

The Doctor Replies, "Ma'am, you had twins: a boy and a girl! Your brother from Maryland came in and named them."

The woman thinks to herself, "No, not my brother...he's an idiot!" She asks the doctor, "Well, what's the girl's name?"

"Denise."

"Wow, that's not a bad name, I like it! What's the boy's name?"

"Denephew."

WHAT DO YOU CALL A GIRL THE NIGHT BEFORE
CHRISTMAS?
Eve.

WHAT DO YOU CALL A BOY WHO ALWAYS
TELLS THE TRUTH?
Frank.

WHAT DO YOU CALL A BOY WHO'S ALL RED
but VERY SWEET?
Barry.

WHAT DO YOU CALL A GIRL WHO LIVES IN A SWAMP?
Marsha.

WHAT DO YOU CALL A BOY STUCK IN A WALL?
Brad.

What do you call a hungry girl?
Late for dinner.

What do you call a girl with lots of purses?
Carrie.

What do you call a girl who always burns dinner?
Charlotte.

What do you call a boy asleep in front of a door?
Matt.

What do you call a boy who never loses a fight?
Victor.

WHAT DO YOU CALL a boy in a POT WITH PEAS,
CARROTS, AND a CHICKEN?

Stu.

WHAT DO YOU CALL a boy being CARRIED
ON HIS MOTHER'S SHOULDER?

Percy.

WHAT DO YOU CALL a MAN WHO ALWAYS CUTS
HIMSELF SHAVING?

Nick.

WHAT DO YOU CALL a GIRL WITH FRESH BREATH
ALL COVERED IN CHOCOLATE?

Peppermint Patty.

A VERY PUNNY STORY
WAIT FOR IT, WAIT FOR IT...

Two Eskimos sitting in a kayak were chilly, but when they lit a fire in the craft, it sank, proving once and for all that you can't have your kayak and heat it, too.

Two boll weevils grew up in South Carolina. One went to Hollywood and became a famous actor. The other stayed behind in the cotton fields and never amounted to much. The second one, naturally, became known as the lesser of two weevils.

A three-legged dog walks into a saloon in the old West. He slides up to the bar and announces: "I'm looking for the man who shot my paw."

A man goes into a restaurant for a Christmas breakfast while visiting his hometown for the holidays. After looking over the menu he says, "I'll just have the eggs Benedict." His order comes a while later and it's served on a big, shiny hubcap. He asks the waiter, "What's with the hubcap?" The waiter sings, "There's no plate like chrome for the hollandaise!"

A neutron goes into a café and asks the waitress, "How much for a soda?" The waitress replies, "For you, no charge."

Two atoms are walking down the street and they run into each other. One says to the other, "Are you all right?" "No, I lost an electron!" says the second atom. "Are you sure?" says the first. The second atom replies, "Yeah, I'm positive!"

A group of chess enthusiasts checked into a hotel and were standing in the lobby discussing their recent tournament victories. After about an hour, the manager came out of the office and asked them to disperse. "But why?" they asked as they moved off. "Because," he said, "I can't stand chess nuts boasting in an open foyer."

THERE WAS A MAN WHO ENTERED A LOCAL PAPER'S PUN CONTEST. HE SENT IN 10 DIFFERENT PUNS IN THE HOPE THAT AT LEAST ONE OF THE PUNS WOULD WIN. UNFORTUNATELY, NO PUN IN TEN DID.

A guy goes to a psychiatrist. "Doc, I keep having these alternating recurring dreams. First I'm a teepee; then I'm a wigwam; then I'm a teepee; then I'm a wigwam. It's driving me crazy. What's wrong with me?" The doctor replies, "It's very simple. You're two tents."

A woman has twins and gives them up for adoption. One of them goes to a family in Egypt and is named Amal. The other goes to a family in Spain; they name him Juan. Years later, Juan sends a picture of himself to his mom. Upon receiving the picture, she tells her husband that she wishes she also had a picture of Amal. Her husband responds: "But they're twins; if you've seen Juan, you've seen Amal."

A pair of chickens walks up to the circulation desk at a public library and say, "Buk Buk BUK." The librarian decides that the chickens desire three books. She gives them the books, and the chickens leave shortly thereafter.

Around midday, the two chickens return to the circulation desk quite vexed and say, "Buk Buk BuKKOOK!" The librarian decides that the chickens desire another three books and hands them over. The chickens leave as before.

The two chickens return to the library in the early afternoon and approach the librarian, looking very annoyed, and say, "Buk Buk Buk Buk Bukkooook!" The librarian is now a little suspicious of these chickens. She gives them what they request, and decides to follow them.

She followed them out of the library, out of the town, and to a park. At this point, she hid behind a tree, not wanting to be seen. She saw the two chickens throwing the books at a frog in a pond, to which the frog was saying, "Rrredit Rrredit Rrredit...."

MIXED NUTS
A GRAB BAG OF RANDOM TEE-HEES

WHAT HAPPENED WHEN THE RED SHIP AND
THE BLUE SHIP COLLIDED?
The survivors were marooned.

WHY ARE ROBOTS NEVER AFRAID?
Because they have nerves of steel.

Lizzie: DID YOU HEAR ABOUT THE WOMAN WHO
CHANGED HER ADDRESS AFTER 65 YEARS?

Emily: Nope.

Lizzie: IT WAS QUITE A MOVING TALE.

WHAT DO YOU CALL A BOOMERANG THAT
DOESN'T WORK?
A stick.

WHAT DID ONE CANDLE SAY TO ANOTHER?
"Are you going out tonight?"

WHY DID THE bike STOP?
It was two-tired.

WHY DID THE MOUNTAIN WISH SHE WAS a VOLCANO?
So she would be more lava-able.

HOW DO YOU CUT THE OCEAN IN HALF?
With a sea saw!

WHY WAS THE NOSE TIRED?
He'd been running all day!

195

Why did King Kong climb the Empire State Building?

Because he couldn't fit in the elevator!

Why don't ghosts like water?

It dampens their spirits!

Why did the boy throw the clock out the window?

He wanted to see time fly.

Where do books sleep?

Under the covers!

What did one toilet say to another toilet?

"You look a bit flushed!"

What's the best thing about numbers?
You can count on them!

Did you hear the Mexican weather report?
Chili today, hot tamale.

What's the fastest country?
Rush-a.

**What state is round on the edges
and high in the middle?**
Ohio!

What state needs glasses?
Mississippi, because it has three Is
and still can't see!

WHy DiD the PicTURe go to JaiL?
He'd been framed!

WHaT DiD the waLL Say to the PicTURe?
"Hang on!"

WHat DiD oNe waLL Say to the oTHeR waLL?
"I'll meet you at the corner!"

WHat DiD the SiDewaLK Say about the
JacKHaMMeR?
"That guy cracks me up!"

WHy aRe SciSSoRS SucH good DanceRS?
Because they can really cut a rug!

When is the best time to bounce on the bed?
Springtime!

What did the cold earring say to the hat?
"Come down ear and cover me up!"

What did one eye say to the other eye?
"Between you and me, something smells!"

What did the chimney say to the roof?
"You really shouldn't smoke!"

Nate: Hello, are you fishing?
Audra: No, I'm drowning worms!

When rain falls, does it ever get up again?
Yes, in dew time.

When you jump down the stairs, does the carpet break your fall?
No, it breaks your leg.

Customer: Waiter, this soup is too hot!
Waiter: That's funny, I thought it was chili!

Bennie: I really like your son.
Mr. Parker: Son? Britney is my daughter!
Bennie: Really? I figured she was a son because she acts like the whole world revolves around her!

Jack: I can't find my skateboard.

Mother: When was the last time you saw it?

Jack: Just before I lost it!

WHEN'S THE BEST TIME TO BUY A BOAT?
When there's a sail on it!

DID YOU HEAR ABOUT THE ELM AND THE
OAK WRESTLING MATCH?
It was a real tree-for-all.

HOW DO YOU MAIL AN ELEPHANT?
In a really big envelope.

HOW DOES A FAT MAN KEEP HIS PANTS UP?
With a conveyor belt.

How much do dead batteries cost?
Nothing—they are free of charge.

A boy walks into a pet shop and sees two tanks of eels. He asks the sales clerk, "What's the difference?"
"The red tank has electric eels from the Pacific Ocean, and the blue tank is full of freshwater eels from Lake Erie."
"How much for the ones in the red tank?"
"A thousand dollars each."
"Wow! How much for the ones in the blue tank?"
"Oh, those are free of charge."

How do you stop a mouse from squeaking?
Oil it.

WHY DO DEER ALWAYS BRING THEIR CHILDREN TO PARTIES?

To make them more fawn.

HOW DO YOU WARM UP A ROOM AFTER IT'S BEEN PAINTED?

Give it a second coat.

WHY WAS THE WATCH FACE RED?

It was ticked off.

WHY DID THE DISH RUN AWAY WITH THE SPOON TO NEW YORK?

To see the Empire Plate Building.

WHAT SHOULD YOU DO if YOU CAN'T
UNLOCK THE DOOR?
Sing until you find the right key!

WHY SHOULD YOU NEVER TELL SECRETS IN
FRONT OF A CLOCK?
Because time will tell.

WHAT DO YOU CALL YOUNG SNOWMEN?
Chilldren.

DID YOU HEAR THE ROPE JOKE?
Just skip it!

HENRY: DID YOU KNOW HE HAD A SET
OF FALSE TEETH?
Frank: Not until it came out in conversation.

WHAT KIND OF PLATES DO SKELETONS USE?
Bone china.

WHAT CAN YOU CATCH FROM YOUR MATTRESS?
Spring fever.

EMILY: Owww! I JUST fell DOWN the STAIRS!
Sydney: Did you have a nice trip?
EMILY: I'LL tell you about it NEXT fall.

LESLEY: I'M SCARED OF LIGHTNING!
Mother: Don't worry! It'll be over in a flash.

What happened to the boat that sank in a lake full of piranhas?
It was left with nothing but a skeleton crew.

Did you hear about the new pirate movie?
It's rated ahhrrrr.

How does a rubber man travel?
In a stretch limo.

What do Alexander the Great and Kermit the Frog have in common?
The same middle name.

206

Did you hear about the fool who always says "No"?

No.

Oh, so it's you!

What did the necktie say to the hat?

"You go on ahead, and I'll just hang around."

What would the U.S. be called if everyone in it drove pink cars?

A pink car-nation!

What would the U.S. be called if everyone lived in their cars?
A re-in-car-nation!

How do you keep your front yard clean?
Take it to the lawn-dro-mat!